Rice Cookbook

An Easy Rice Cookbook with 50 Delicious Rice Recipes

By
BookSumo Press

Published by
http://www.booksumo.com

LEGAL NOTES

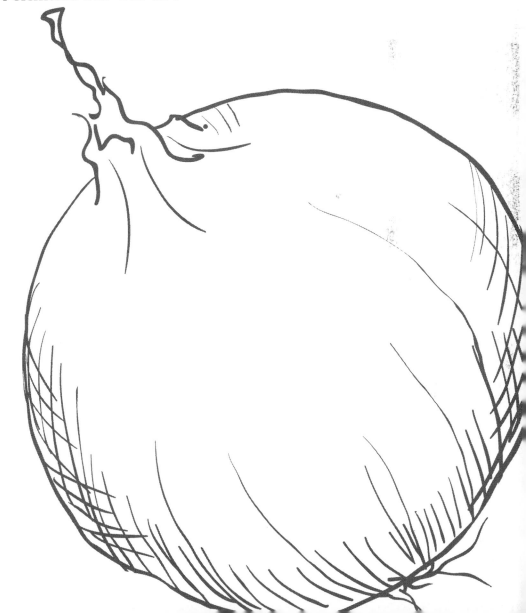

Table of Contents

Latin Style Rice 44

Easy Persian Style Rice 45

Bacon, Apples, and Mushroom White Rice 46

Basmati Peas and Peanut Rice 47

Latin Style Rice 48

West African Style Rice 49

Chili and Cilantro Jasmine 50

Texas Ranch Style Basmati 51

Punjabi Style Spicy Meatballs with Basmati 52

Basmati Marrakesh 53

Caribbean Basmati Salad 54

Hot Sweet and Savory Basmati with Figs 55

Country Style Mushroom Basmati 56

Southern Italian Style Basmati with Tomato Base 57

Arizona Basmati 58

Tuesday's Buttery Almond Basmati 59

20-Minute Rice Cooker Basmati 60

Vermicelli Pilaf 61

Peppery Pecan Basmati with Mushrooms 62

Milanese Basmati 63

Bashir's Basmati Pudding 64

European Cabbage Rolls 65

Turkey Basmati Bake 67

Persian Pomegranate Rice Salad 68

Cinnamon Sugar Basmati 69

American Basmati Chili 70

3-Ingredient Cajun Basmati 72

Full Basmati Rice Platter 73

30-Minute Basmati Pilaf 74

Azza's Basmati Salad 75

Ginger Basmati with Eggplant 76

Karachi Style Chicken Salad 77

Basmati Kerala 78

Ginger Garlic Basmati with Squash 79

60-Minute Basmati 80

Topical Chutney with Basmati 81

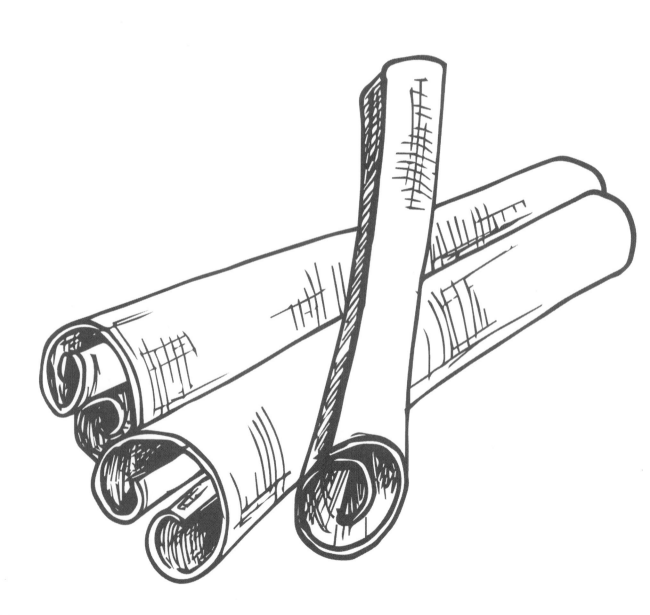

West African Dinner (Jollof Rice with Chicken)

🍲 Prep Time: 2 hrs
🕐 Total Time: 2 hrs

Servings per Recipe: 6
Calories	479.2
Fat	25.9g
Cholesterol	103.5mg
Sodium	556.7mg
Carbohydrates	29.9g
Protein	29.7g

Ingredients

3 lbs. chicken pieces
2 tbsp oil
1 medium onion, chopped
16 ounces canned tomatoes, cut up
1 1/4 C. chicken broth
1 bay leaf
1/2 tsp ground ginger
1/2 tsp cinnamon

1/2 tsp thyme, crushed
1/2 tsp salt
1/4 tsp ground red pepper
1 C. long grain rice
1 tbsp parsley, chopped

Directions

1. Place a pan over medium heat. Heat in it the oil. Cook in it the chicken pieces for 6 to 7 min on each side.
2. Drain the chicken pieces and place them aside.
3. Stir the onion into the remaining oil in the skillet. Cook it for 4 min. Drain it the onion and discard the remaining oil.
4. Stir the chicken back with onion into skillet with undrained tomatoes, broth, and seasonings.
5. Let them cook until they start boiling. Lower the heat and put on the lid. Let the stew cook for 32 min.
6. Discard the fat that rise on top. Stir the rice into the pan. Put on the lid and let them cook for 32 min.
7. Once the time is up, drain the bay lead and discard.
8. Garnish your chicken rice skillet with some parsley then serve it.
9. Enjoy.

MOROCCAN
Pilaf

 Prep Time: 15 mins

Total Time: 45 mins

Servings per Recipe: 4

Calories	586.4
Fat	16.6 g
Cholesterol	23.3mg
Sodium	746.7mg
Carbohydrates	92.1g
Protein	14.9 g

Ingredients

2 C. long grain rice
2 tbsp butter
2 tbsp olive oil
1 onion, chopped
2 garlic cloves, chopped
1 - 2 cinnamon stick
1/2 tsp salt
1/2 tsp ginger
1/2 tsp white pepper
1/2 tsp cumin

1/2 tsp turmeric
1/4 C. fresh cilantro, chopped
1/4 C. peas
1 red bell pepper, chopped
1 carrot, chopped
4 1/2 C. chicken stock
1/4 tsp saffron thread, crushed

Directions

1. Place a large saucepan over high heat. Heat in it the stock until it starts boiling.
2. In the meantime, place a deep skillet over medium heat. Stir in it the rest of the ingredients aside for the saffron. Let them cook for 11 min.
3. Stir the saffron with boiling stock into the rice pan.
4. Let them cook for 5 min. Put on the lid and cook them for 26 min until the rice is done
5. Serve your rice skillet warm with some leftover chicken.
6. Enjoy.

Easy
Chicken Curry with Rice

Prep Time: 10 mins
Total Time: 1 hr 20 mins

Servings per Recipe: 6
Calories	564 kcal
Fat	22.2 g
Carbohydrates	58g
Protein	32 g
Cholesterol	83 mg
Sodium	631 mg

Ingredients

2 tbsp curry powder
1 tsp ground ginger
1/2 tsp ground cinnamon
1/4 tsp ground cloves
1/4 tsp cayenne pepper
2 tbsp vegetable oil
1 large onion, halved and thinly sliced
3 garlic cloves, minced
1 rotisserie chicken, skinned and boned,
meat pulled into large chunks

1 (13.5 oz.) can light coconut milk
1 (14.5 oz.) can diced tomatoes
1 (14.5 oz.) can chicken broth
To serve:
Cooked basmati rice
chopped fresh cilantro
mango chutney

Directions

1. In a small bowl, mix together all the spices.
2. In a Dutch oven, heat the oil on medium-high heat and sauté the onion for about 8-10 minutes.
3. Add the garlic and sauté for about 30 seconds.
4. Add the spice mixture and sauté for about 30-60 seconds.
5. Stir in the chicken, coconut milk, tomatoes and broth and bring to a boil.
6. Reduce the heat and cook, uncovered for about 20 minutes.
7. Remove from the heat and sprinkle with the cilantro.
8. Serve over the rice alongside the chutney.

FRIED RICE
for Thursday Nights

 Prep Time: 15 mins

Total Time: 35 mins

Servings per Recipe: 6

Calories	315 kcal
Fat	13.1 g
Carbohydrates	28.1g
Protein	20.1 g
Cholesterol	128 mg
Sodium	559 mg

Ingredients

3 tbsp vegetable oil, divided

3 eggs, beaten

3 C. cold, cooked white rice

2 C. chopped cooked chicken

1/2 C. sliced celery

1/2 C. shredded carrot

1 C. frozen green peas, thawed

2 green onions, sliced

3 tbsp soy sauce

Directions

1. In a large skillet, heat 1 tbsp of the oil on medium-high heat and cook the eggs till scrambled.

2. Transfer the scrambled eggs into a plate and keep aside.

3. In the same skillet, heat remaining 2 tbsp of the oil on high heat and stir in the rice.

4. Add the chicken, celery, carrot, peas and green onions and stir to combine.

5. Reduce the heat to medium and cook, covered for about 5 minutes.

6. Stir in the scrambled eggs and soy sauce and cook till heated completely.

Yuki's
Shrimp Fried Rice

🥣 Prep Time: 30 mins
🕐 Total Time: 1 hr

Servings per Recipe: 4
Calories	553 kcal
Fat	22.8 g
Carbohydrates	61.2g
Protein	26.4 g
Cholesterol	375 mg
Sodium	1209 mg

Ingredients

2 tbsp olive oil
1 carrot, diced
1/2 green bell pepper, diced
2 C. shrimp, peeled and deveined
1/2 onion, diced
1/2 (15.25 oz.) can whole kernel corn, drained
2 cloves garlic, thinly sliced
1 tbsp olive oil
2 eggs, beaten

4 C. cooked rice, cooled
2 tbsp oyster sauce
2 tbsp soy sauce
1 tbsp butter
1/2 tsp salt
1 tsp butter
4 eggs, divided

Directions

1. In a large skillet, heat 2 tbsp of the olive oil on medium heat and cook the carrot and green bell pepper for about 5 minutes.
2. Stir in the shrimp, onion, corn and garlic and cook for about 5 minutes.
3. Discard any liquid from the skillet.
4. Reduce the heat to low and let mixture simmer.
5. In another skillet, heat 1 tbsp of the olive oil on medium heat and cook 2 beaten eggs 2-3 minutes, stirring continuously.
6. Add the oyster sauce, soy sauce, 1 tbsp of the butter and salt and toss to coat.
7. In a small nonstick skillet, melt 1 tsp of the butter on medium heat.
8. Carefully, break 1 of the remaining eggs in the skillet and cook, covered for about 3 minutes.
9. Transfer the egg into a plate and keep aside.
10. Repeat with the remaining 3 eggs.
11. Transfer the rice into a serving plate and serve with a topping of the fried eggs.

HOW TO MAKE
Fried Rice

Prep Time: 25 mins
Total Time: 2 hrs 38 mins

Servings per Recipe: 4
Calories	493 kcal
Fat	17.2 g
Carbohydrates	55.4g
Protein	27 g
Cholesterol	161 mg
Sodium	1214 mg

Ingredients

1 lb. boneless chicken thighs, cut into
1/3-inch pieces across the grain
2 tbsp light soy sauce
2 tbsp brown sugar
1/4 tsp ground black pepper
2 tbsp vegetable oil
1/4 C. chopped onion
4 cloves garlic, chopped
2 eggs, beaten
3 tbsp light soy sauce

1 tsp white sugar
1 tsp ground white pepper
4 C. leftover cooked rice
1/4 C. thinly sliced green onions
1/4 C. chopped cilantro

Directions

1. In a bowl, mix together the chicken thighs, 2 tbsp of the soy sauce, brown sugar and black pepper. Refrigerate, covered for about 2 hours to overnight. In a very large skillet, heat the vegetable oil on high heat. Reduce the heat to medium and sauté the onion and garlic for about 2 minutes. Increase the heat to high and cook the marinated chicken for about 4 minutes, stirring continuously.
2. Push the chicken mixture to one side of the skillet.
3. Place the eggs into the empty side and cook for about 2 minutes, stirring continuously.
4. Stir in the chicken mixture, 3 tbsp of the soy sauce, sugar and white pepper and cook for about 1 minute.
5. Stir in the rice and cook for about 4 minutes.
6. Remove from heat and gently, stir in the green onion and cilantro.

Fried Rice
Lunch Box

🥣 Prep Time: 15 mins
🕐 Total Time: 1 hr 45 mins

Servings per Recipe: 4

Calories	302 kcal
Fat	11.3 g
Carbohydrates	45.5g
Protein	4.7 g
Cholesterol	0 mg
Sodium	550 mg

Ingredients

1 C. uncooked jasmine rice
1/2 C. water
3 tbsp vegetable oil
2 cloves garlic, minced
2 tbsp chopped carrot
1 tbsp chopped onion
3 tbsp soy-based liquid seasoning
1/4 C. reduced-soy sauce
2 tbsp chopped green onion
1 tbsp chopped cashews

1 tsp raisins
1/4 tsp white sugar
1/4 tsp white pepper
5 canned lychees, drained and quartered

Directions

1. In a pan, add the rice and water on high heat and bring to a boil.
2. Reduce heat to medium-low and simmer, covered for about 20-25 minutes.
3. Transfer the rice into a shallow dish and refrigerate till cold.
4. In large skillet, heat the oil on medium-high heat and sauté the garlic for a few seconds.
5. Add the carrots and onion and cooking till the onion begins to soften.
6. Stir in the cold rice and cook till heated completely.
7. Stir in the soy sauce, soy seasoning, green onions, cashews, raisins, salt and white pepper and cook till heated completely.
8. Stir in the quartered lychees and serve.

KOREAN
Chicken Cutlets and Fried Rice

 Prep Time: 20 mins
Total Time: 38 mins

Servings per Recipe: 2
Calories	824 kcal
Fat	47.4 g
Carbohydrates	64.6g
Protein	33.6 g
Cholesterol	97 mg
Sodium	1884 mg

Ingredients

2 skin-on, boneless chicken breasts
salt and ground black pepper to taste
1/4 C. peanut oil, divided
1/4 C. Korean barbecue sauce
1 slice fully cooked luncheon meat, cubed
1 tbsp butter
1/2 C. chopped Napa cabbage kimchee
1/4 C. chopped pickled carrot and daikon radish
2 C. cooked white rice, cooled

1 tbsp soy-based liquid seasoning
2 tsp soy sauce
1 tbsp dried garlic flakes
2 tbsp gochujang (Korean hot pepper paste)
1 tbsp mayonnaise
1 tsp Sriracha hot sauce
1 green onion, chopped

Directions

1. Place the chicken breasts onto a smooth surface and with a meat mallet, pound into an even thickness.
2. Season with the salt and pepper and coat with 2 tbsp of the peanut oil evenly.
3. Heat a heavy skillet on medium heat and cook the chicken for about 4 minutes per side.
4. Coat the the top of the chicken with the barbecue sauce and cook, covered for about 1 minute per side.
5. Transfer chicken into a plate and cover with a piece of the foil to keep warm.
6. With a paper towel, wipe the skillet.
7. In the same skillet, heat remaining 2 tbsp of the peanut oil on medium heat and cook the luncheon meat for about 3-5 minutes.
8. In another skillet, melt the butter on medium heat and cook the pickled carrot, daikon, kimchee and rice for about 1-2 minutes.
9. Stir in the liquid seasoning, soy sauce and garlic flakes and cook for about 3-5 minutes.

16

10. Add the gochujang and luncheon meat into rice mixture and mix well.
11. Cut the chicken into desired slices.
12. In a small bowl, mix together the mayonnaise and Sriracha hot sauce.
13. Divide the fried rice into serving plates and top with the chicken slices.
14. Place the mayonnaise mixture over the chicken and serve with a garnishing of the green onion on top.

AMERICAN
Fried Rice

Prep Time: 10 mins
Total Time: 40 mins

Servings per Recipe: 4
Calories	431 kcal
Fat	17.3 g
Carbohydrates	58.5g
Protein	11.8 g
Cholesterol	217 mg
Sodium	837 mg

Ingredients

1 C. uncooked white rice
2 C. water
1/2 C. diced carrots
1/2 C. diced onion
4 tbsp butter or margarine, divided
4 eggs

2 tbsp milk
1 C. ketchup
salt and pepper to taste

Directions

1. In a small pan, add the rice and water and bring to a boil.
2. Reduce the heat to low and simmer, covered for about 15-20 minutes.
3. In a large skillet, melt 1 tbsp of the butter on medium heat and cook the carrots and onion for about 5 minutes, stirring occasionally.
4. Add the cooked rice and stir to combine.
5. Stir in the remaining butter and reduce the heat to medium-low.
6. Stir in the ketchup and simmer for about 5 minutes.
7. Remove from the heat.
8. In a small bowl, add the eggs and milk and beat till well combined.
9. Heat a nonstick skillet on medium heat and cook half of the egg mixture till firm, flipping once in the middle way.
10. Transfer the cooked egg into a plate and cut in half.
11. Repeat with the remaining egg mixture.
12. Transfer the rice into a serving plate and serve with a topping of the egg halves.

Fried Rice
Rice Glitter

Prep Time: 15 mins
Total Time: 25 mins

Servings per Recipe: 6

Calories	274 kcal
Fat	14.2 g
Carbohydrates	32.8g
Protein	2.5 g
Cholesterol	0 mg
Sodium	195 mg

Ingredients

3 C. cooked rice
2 tsp garlic powder
2 tsp onion powder
salt and ground black pepper to taste
2 tbsp grapeseed oil
1/2 red bell pepper, chopped
1/2 carrot, chopped

1/2 stalk celery, chopped
1/4 C. water
1/2 C. French-fried onions

Directions

1. In a large bowl, mix together the rice, garlic powder, onion powder, salt and black pepper.
2. In a large skillet, heat the oil on medium heat and cook the red bell pepper, carrot and celery for about 5 minutes.
3. Add the seasoned rice and water and cook for about 5 minutes.
4. Add the French-fried onions and toss to coat.

NEON
Fried Rice

🍲 Prep Time: 15 mins
🕐 Total Time: 25 mins

Servings per Recipe: 6
Calories	277.8
Fat	9.8g
Cholesterol	98.0mg
Sodium	723.8mg
Carbohydrates	38.6g
Protein	7.6g

Ingredients

3 eggs
1 tbsp water
1 tbsp butter
2 - 3 tbsp oil
1 medium onion, finely chopped
3 garlic cloves, coarsely chopped

4 C. cold cooked white rice
4 tbsp soy sauce
1 tsp sesame oil
1/2 tsp fresh ground black pepper
2 green onions, finely chopped

Directions

1. In a small bowl, add the eggs and water and beat well.
2. In a large skillet, melt the butter on medium heat.
3. Add the eggs mixture and cook for about 2 minutes, without stirring.
4. Transfer the omelet into a plate and then chop it.
5. In the same skillet, heat the oil and sauté the onion for about 2 minutes.
6. Add the garlic and sauté for about 2 minutes.
7. Stir in the cold rice, soy sauce, sesame oil and black pepper and stir fry for about 5 minutes.
8. Stir in the egg and green onion and serve hot.

Hibachi
Fried Rice

Prep Time: 5 mins
Total Time: 40 mins

Servings per Recipe: 4
Calories   356.5
Fat   7.2g1
Cholesterol   104.4mg
Sodium   616.0mg
Carbohydrates   60.6g
Protein   10.5g

Ingredients

4 C. cooked rice
1 C. frozen peas, thawed
2 tbsp carrots, finely diced
2 eggs, beaten
1/2 C. onion, diced
1 1/2 tbsp butter
2 tbsp soy sauce

salt
pepper

Directions

1. In a pan, add 2 C. of the water and a pinch of the salt and bring to a boil.
2. Stir in the rice and reduce the heat to low.
3. Simmer, covered for about 20 minutes.
4. Transfer the rice into a large bowl and refrigerate to cool.
5. In a small pan, add the eggs on medium heat and cook till scrambled, breaking into small pieces.
6. After cooling, remove the bowl of rice from the refrigerator.
7. In the bowl of rice, add peas, grated carrot, scrambled egg and diced onion and gently, toss to coat.
8. In a large frying pan, melt the butter on medium-high heat and cook the rice mixture with the soy sauce, a pinch of salt and pepper for about 6-8 minutes, stirring occasionally.

FRIED RICE
in Jakarta

Prep Time: 15 mins
Total Time: 25 mins

Servings per Recipe: 6
Calories	382.9
Fat	9.8g
Cholesterol	129.2mg
Sodium	497.9mg2
Carbohydrates	53.1g
Protein	18.3g

Ingredients

2 C. uncooked long-grain white rice
2 eggs, beaten
2 tsp sesame oil
1/2 tsp salt
8 oz. boneless skinless chicken thighs,
cut into 1/2 inch strips
6 oz. raw shrimp, peeled
2 tbsp vegetable oil
2 tbsp chopped garlic
1 medium onion, finely chopped
2 tsp finely chopped fresh ginger root

1 tbsp dried shrimp paste
1/2 tsp fresh ground black pepper
1 tbsp chili bean sauce
1 tbsp oyster sauce
1 tbsp dark soy sauce
Toppings
3 tbsp finely chopped spring onions
1/2 C. fresh cilantro leaves, chopped

Directions

1. In a large pan of salted water, cook the rice till tender.
2. Drain the rice and spread onto a baking sheet to cool for at least 2 hours.
3. In a bowl, add the eggs, sesame oil and salt and beat till well combined.
4. I a large frying pan, heat the oil till slightly smoking and stir fry the onions, ginger, shrimp paste, garlic and pepper for about 2 minutes, squashing the shrimp paste.
5. Stir in the chicken and shrimp and stir fry for about 2 minutes.
6. Stir in the rice and stir fry for about 3 minutes.
7. Stir in the chili bean sauce, oyster sauce and soy sauce and stir fry for about 2 minutes.
8. Stir in the egg mixture and stir fry for about 1 minute.
9. Serve hot with a garnishing of the spring onion and fresh cilantro.

Hawaiian
Fried Rice II

🍲 Prep Time: 15 mins
🕐 Total Time: 40 mins

Servings per Recipe: 8
Calories	532.0
Fat	5.0g
Cholesterol	139.5mg
Sodium	2222.7mg
Carbohydrates	102.6g
Protein	17.5g

Ingredients

4 1/2 C. dry rice, cooked and cooled
6 -7 eggs, with a splash water, scrambled
1 (11 oz.) cans Spam lite, diced
1 yellow onion, diced
12 oz. frozen peas and carrots, thawed
Sauce
1 C. aloha shoyu soy sauce

6 -7 tbsp for Kikkoman soy sauce
4 -5 garlic cloves, minced
2 tbsp oyster sauce
1 tsp sesame oil

Directions

1. In a wok, heat 1/2 tbsp of the vegetable oil on medium-high heat and cook the eggs till scrambled.
2. Transfer the scrambled eggs into a bowl.
3. In the same wok, heat 1 tbsp of the oil on medium-high heat and sauté the onions and Spam till golden and starts to crisp.
4. Meanwhile in a bowl, add all the sauce ingredients and stir till the sugar dissolves.
5. Stir in the thawed peas, carrots and sauce mixture and bring to a boil on high heat.
6. Cook till the mixture changes into a glaze.
7. Slowly, add the cooled rice and eggs, breaking up any clumps of rice and cook till heated completely. Serve immediately.

AMERICAN
Mediterranean Fried Rice

 Prep Time: 15 mins

Total Time: 45 mins

Servings per Recipe: 6
Calories	197.1
Fat	5.7g
Cholesterol	76.8mg
Sodium	479.3mg
Carbohydrates	28.4g
Protein	6.8g

Ingredients

1 C. rice, uncooked
1 - 2 C. chicken stock
2 - 3 slices bacon, cooked & chopped
2 tbsp shallots (green onions)
1 C. prawns, cooked
2 eggs

1 tbsp lemon juice
2 - 3 tbsp soy sauce

Directions

1. Grease a pan with a little olive oil and cook the eggs till set, breaking the yolks with the knife.
2. Then, cut the eggs into small strips and transfer into a bowl.
3. Add the rice and cook till browned.
4. Add the stock and cook till all the moisture is absorbed.
5. Add the shallots, egg, bacon pieces and cooked prawns and cook till heated completely.
6. Stir in the lemon juice and soy sauce and remove from the heat.

Lime
Fried Rice with Prawns

Prep Time: 15 mins
Total Time: 25 mins

Servings per Recipe: 4
Calories	379.2
Fat	7.3g
Cholesterol	234.7mg
Sodium	1364.6mg
Carbohydrates	50.9g
Protein	23.7g

Ingredients

2 eggs, lightly beaten
1 (450 g) bags shrimp, frozen, raw, thawed
1 tbsp sesame oil
2 spring onions, sliced
1 garlic clove, crushed
1/2 C. Thai sweet chili sauce, sweet
1 tbsp dark soy sauce
1 tbsp fish sauce
lime juice
3 C. cooked rice
100 g snow peas, trimmed, thinly sliced

Directions

1. Heat a lightly greased frying pan and cook the beaten eggs for about 1-2 minutes.
2. Transfer the omelet onto a chopping board and keep aside to cool.
3. Roll the omelet and cut into thin slices.
4. With the paper towels, pat dry the prawns.
5. In a deep frying pan, heat the sesame oil and cook the prawns till they turn pink. Transfer the prawns into a bowl.
6. Cover with a piece of the foil to keep warm and keep aside.
7. In the same pan, add the spring onions and garlic on medium heat and stir-fry for about 1 minute.
8. Stir in the sweet chills sauce, soma sauce, fish sauce, lime juice, prawns, cooked rice and snow peas and toss to coat well.
9. Stir fry till the rice and prawns are heated completely.
10. Gently, stir in the omelet slices and serve.

KING
Fried Rice

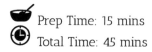 Prep Time: 15 mins

Total Time: 45 mins

Servings per Recipe: 4

Calories	915.9
Fat	21.8g
Cholesterol	158.6mg
Sodium	1188.1mg
Carbohydrates	156.0g
Protein	19.5g

Ingredients

4 C. jasmine rice, cooked and cooled
1 C. crabmeat, shredded
1/4 C. cooking oil
1/4 C. soy sauce
3 eggs, beaten
3 tbsp green onions, finely chopped

1 tbsp sesame oil
2 garlic cloves, finely chopped
2 tsp black pepper, ground
2 tsp sugar
1 tsp Thai fish sauce

Directions

1. In a bowl, mix together the sugar, pepper, soy sauce and fish sauce.
2. In a large frying pan, heat the oil on medium heat and lightly, sauté the garlic and green onion.
3. Add the rice and mix till well combined.
4. Add the egg and cook till done.
5. Stir in the crab meat and cook till well combined, breaking up the clumps.
6. Add the sauce mixture and mix well.
7. Serve immediately.

Arizona
Fried Rice

Prep Time: 10 mins

Total Time: 50 mins

Servings per Recipe: 6

Calories	255.4
Fat	3.4g
Cholesterol	43.8mg
Sodium	444.3mg
Carbohydrates	34.2g
Protein	22.5g

Ingredients

1 lb boneless skinless chicken breast, cubed
1 (10 oz.) packages frozen corn, thawed
1 small green pepper, chopped
1 small onion, shopped
2 tsp canola oil
1 C. chicken broth

1 C. salsa
1 tsp chili powder
1/4 tsp cayenne pepper
1 1/2 C. uncooked instant rice
1/2 shredded low-fat cheddar cheese

Directions

1. In a large nonstick skillet, heat the oil and sauté the chicken, corn, green pepper and onion till the chicken becomes golden brown.
2. Stir in the broth, salsa, chili powder and cayenne pepper and bring to a boil.
3. Add the rice and stir to combine well.
4. Cover the skillet and immediately, remove from the heat.
5. Keep aside, covered for about 5 minutes.
6. With a fork, fluff the rice and sprinkle with the cheddar cheese.
7. Keep aside, covered for about 2-3 minutes.

ASIAN
Fusion Fried Rice

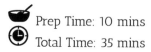 Prep Time: 10 mins

Total Time: 35 mins

Servings per Recipe: 4

Calories	371.8
Fat	11.8g
Cholesterol	270.6mg
Sodium	659.1mg
Carbohydrates	39.7g
Protein	25.3g

Ingredients

4 chicken drumsticks
2 tbsp fresh ginger, grated
2 tbsp soy sauce
2 large carrots, chopped
15 oz. cooked rice
8 oz. sugar snap peas

1/2 C. red pepper, chopped
4 eggs, beaten
green onion, sliced for garnish
soy sauce, for garnish
toasted sesame oil (to garnish)

Directions

1. In a large skillet, heat 1 tbsp of the oil on medium-high heat and sear the chicken with half of the ginger and soy sauce till browned from all the sides.
2. Add 1/2 C. of the water and cook, covered for about 15 minutes.
3. Meanwhile in a microwave safe bowl, add the carrots, remaining ginger and 2 tbsp of the water and microwave on High for about 4 minutes.
4. Add the rice, peas, red pepper and microwave, covered for about 5 minutes, stirring twice.
5. Remove the chicken and juices from the skillet and transfer into a bowl.
6. With paper towels, wipe dry the skillet.
7. In the same skillet, add the eggs and cook for about 3-4 minutes or till scrambled. Stir in the rice mixture and cook till heated completely.
8. Serve ye chicken with the fried rice and serve with a topping of the green onions, soy sauce and sesame oil.

Ground Beef
Fried Rice

🥣 Prep Time: 10 mins
🕐 Total Time: 40 mins

Servings per Recipe: 6

Calories	315 kcal
Fat	13.1
Carbohydrates	28.1g
Protein	20.1g
Cholesterol	128mg
Sodium	559 mg

Ingredients

3 tbsp vegetable oil, divided
3 eggs, beaten
3 C. cold, cooked white rice
2 C. chopped cooked ground beef
1/2 C. sliced mushrooms
1/2 C. shredded carrot
1 C. frozen green peas, thawed

2 green onions, sliced
3 tbsp soy sauce

Directions

1. In a large skillet, heat 1 tbsp of the oil on medium-high heat and cook the eggs till scrambled.
2. Transfer the scrambled eggs into a plate and keep aside.
3. In the same skillet, heat remaining 2 tbsp of the oil on high heat and stir in the rice.
4. Add the ground beef, mushrooms, carrot, peas and green onions and stir to combine.
5. Reduce the heat to medium and cook, covered for about 5 minutes.
6. Stir in the scrambled eggs and soy sauce and cook till heated completely.

FRIED RICE
with Almonds

 Prep Time: 10 mins

Total Time: 40 mins

Servings per Recipe: 4

Calories	356.5
Fat	7.2g1
Cholesterol	104.4mg
Sodium	616.0mg
Carbohydrates	60.6g
Protein	10.5g

Ingredients

4 C. cooked rice
1 C. frozen peas, thawed
2 tbsp almonds, finely diced
2 eggs, beaten
1/2 C. onion, diced
1 1/2 tbsp butter

2 tbsp soy sauce
salt
pepper

Directions

1. In a pan, add 2 C. of the water and a pinch of the salt and bring to a boil.
2. Stir in the rice and reduce the heat to low.
3. Simmer, covered for about 20 minutes.
4. Transfer the rice into a large bowl and refrigerate to cool.
5. In a small pan, add the eggs on medium heat and cook till scrambled, breaking into small pieces.
6. After cooling, remove the bowl of rice from the refrigerator.
7. In the bowl of rice, add peas, almonds, scrambled egg and diced onion and gently, toss to coat.
8. In a large frying pan, melt the butter on medium-high heat and cook the rice mixture with the soy sauce, a pinch of salt and pepper for about 6-8 minutes, stirring occasionally.

Sage
and Black Bean Brown Rice

🥣 Prep Time: 15 mins
🕐 Total Time: 1 hr 55 mins

Servings per Recipe: 10

Calories	101 kcal
Fat	1.2 g
Carbohydrates	15.4g
Protein	6.8 g
Cholesterol	14 mg
Sodium	759 mg

Ingredients

5 C. chicken broth
2 skinless, boneless chicken breast halves
1 C. diced celery
1 C. diced onion
1/4 C. diced carrots
1/4 C. corn
1/4 C. drained and rinsed black beans

1 tsp dried sage
1 tsp ground black pepper
1 tsp salt
1 bay leaf
3/4 C. brown rice

Directions

1. Get your broth boiling and cook the chicken in it for 22 mins.
2. Then place the chicken to the side before shredding it.
3. Add the following to the boiling broth: bay leaves, chicken, salt, rice, celery, pepper, onions, sage, carrots, black beans, and corn.
4. Let the contents continue to cook for 60 more mins. Then serve after letting it sit for 12 to 15 mins.
5. Enjoy.

EASY MOROCCAN
Style Brown Rice

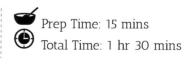

Prep Time: 15 mins
Total Time: 1 hr 30 mins

Servings per Recipe: 6

Calories	681 kcal
Fat	23.1 g
Carbohydrates	82.2g
Protein	36.6 g
Cholesterol	97 mg
Sodium	1425 mg

Ingredients

1/2 C. soy sauce
1/2 C. fresh lemon juice
1/2 C. sherry
1/2 C. honey
1/2 tsp ground thyme
2 tsps curry powder
1/2 tsp dried oregano
1/2 tsp ground ginger
1/2 tsp ground black pepper
1 clove garlic, pressed

3 lbs cut up chicken pieces
1 1/2 C. uncooked brown rice
3 C. water
2 tbsps olive oil
8 pitted prunes
8 dried apricot halves

Directions

1. Place your chicken in a bowl with the following: garlic, soy sauce, black pepper, lemon juice, ginger, sherry, oregano, honey, curry, and thyme.
2. Place a covering of plastic wrap around the bowl and marinate it in the fridge for 60 mins to overnight (longer is better).
3. Get your water and rice boiling, then place a lid on the pot, let the contents cook for 47 mins with a low level of heat.
4. Stir fry your chicken in olive oil until fully browned then add in apricots and prunes.
5. Cook for 1 more min before pouring in the marinade.
6. Let the contents lightly boil with a low to medium level of heat until the chicken is fully done for about 17 mins.
7. Enjoy the rice with a topping of chicken.

Peppers and Honey Brown Rice

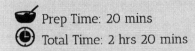 Prep Time: 20 mins
🕐 Total Time: 2 hrs 20 mins

Servings per Recipe: 8
Calories	203 kcal
Fat	6.9 g
Carbohydrates	30.5g
Protein	5.5 g
Cholesterol	14 mg
Sodium	143 mg

Ingredients

1 2/3 C. uncooked brown rice
2 1/2 C. water
1 C. low fat sour cream
1 tbsp red wine vinegar
1 tbsp fresh lime juice
2 tsps honey
1/2 tsp ground cumin
1/4 tsp chili powder
1/4 tsp salt
1/8 tsp black pepper

2 slices bacon
1 C. diced red bell pepper
1 C. chopped green onions
1/2 C. frozen green peas, thawed
1/4 C. toasted almond slices
2 tbsps chopped cilantro

Directions

1. Boil your water and rice and the place a lid on the pot, set the heat to low and let the contents cook for 47 mins then let it cool, and stir it.
2. Pour the rice in a bowl, and add to the bowl: pepper, sour cream, salt, vinegar, chili powder, lime juice, cumin, and honey.
3. Place the mix in the fridge after stirring and then fry your bacon and break it into pieces.
4. Get a bigger bowl, and combine: cilantro, rice, almonds, dressing, peas, bacon, onions, and bell peppers.
5. Place everything back in the fridge for 60 mins.
6. Enjoy.

BACKROAD STYLE
Brown Rice

Prep Time: 20 mins
Total Time: 1 hr 50 mins

Servings per Recipe: 15
Calories	170 kcal
Fat	9.1 g
Carbohydrates	18.7g
Protein	4.5 g
Cholesterol	17 mg
Sodium	283 mg

Ingredients

cooking spray
1/2 C. butter
1 C. uncooked wild rice
3/4 C. uncooked brown rice
6 green onions, chopped
1 (8 oz.) package sliced mushrooms

1 (2.25 oz.) package slivered almonds
1 (10.5 oz.) can condensed French onion soup
1 (10.5 oz.) can beef consommé

Directions

1. Coat a casserole dish with nonstick spray and then set your oven to 350 degrees before doing anything else.
2. Toast your brown & wild rice in butter for 7 mins then add in the onions and cook for 4 more mins before adding the almonds, consommé, soup, and mushrooms.
3. Pour everything into your casserole dish and place a covering of foil around it. Cook the contents it in the oven for 75 mins.
4. Then stir everything.
5. Enjoy.

Easy
Mexican Style Brown Rice II

🍲 Prep Time: 20 mins
🕐 Total Time: 2 hrs 20 mins

Servings per Recipe: 8	
Calories	397 kcal
Fat	22.6 g
Carbohydrates	42.4g
Protein	9.1 g
Cholesterol	0 mg
Sodium	532 mg

Ingredients

2 C. cooked quinoa
1 (15 oz.) can pinto beans, rinsed and drained
1 (15 oz.) can kidney beans, rinsed and drained
1 (14 oz.) can corn
1 red onion, chopped
1 C. cooked brown rice
1 red bell pepper, chopped
1/4 C. chopped fresh cilantro

Dressing:
3/4 C. olive oil
1/3 C. red wine vinegar
1 tbsp chili powder, or to taste
2 cloves garlic, mashed
1/2 tsp salt
1/2 tsp ground black pepper
1/4 tsp cayenne pepper, or to taste

Directions

1. Get a bowl, combine: cilantro, quinoa, bell peppers, beans, rice, corn, and onions.
2. Get a 2nd bowl, combine: black and cayenne pepper, olive oil, garlic, vinegar, and chili powder.
3. Combine both bowls, then stir the mixture.
4. Place a covering over the bowl and leave it in the fridge for at least 60 mins before serving.
5. Enjoy.

BROWN RICE
and Black Bean Burgers

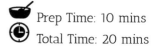 Prep Time: 10 mins

Total Time: 20 mins

Servings per Recipe: 4

Calories	484 kcal
Fat	9.5 g
Carbohydrates	75g
Protein	24.4 g
Cholesterol	58 mg
Sodium	1192 mg

Ingredients

1 (15 oz.) can black beans, rinsed and drained
1 C. cooked brown rice
1 small onion, finely chopped
1 egg, lightly beaten
1 C. bread crumbs
2 tbsps salsa

1/4 C. reduced-fat sour cream
1/4 C. salsa
4 hamburger buns, split
4 lettuce leaves
4 slices reduced-fat Cheddar cheese

Directions

1. Get a bowl and mash your beans in it. Then add in: salsa (2 tbsps), rice, bread crumbs, eggs, and onions.
2. Form half a C. of the mixture into patties then fry them in oil for 4 mins for each side.
3. Get a 2nd bowl, combine: salsa (4 tbsps), and sour cream.
4. Layer the following on your bun: a patty, cheddar, salsa mix, and lettuce.
5. Do this for the remaining contents.
6. Enjoy.

Cilantro and Tea Brown Rice

Prep Time: 5 mins
Total Time: 1 hr

Servings per Recipe: 6

Calories	150 kcal
Fat	2.9 g
Carbohydrates	27.9 g
Protein	2.8 g
Cholesterol	5 mg
Sodium	20 mg

Ingredients

3 C. water
1 jasmine herbal tea bag
1 cube vegetable bouillon
1 1/2 C. uncooked brown rice

1 tbsp butter
2 tbsps chopped fresh cilantr

Directions

1. Boil your water with the tea bag as well.
2. Then take out the tea bag after 2 mins of boiling.
3. Add the bouillon and the rice.
4. Get everything boiling again, before placing a lid on the pot, setting the heat to low, and cooking the mix for 47 mins.
5. Shut the heat and once the rice has cooled off a bit stir it and add in your butter.
6. When serving add a garnishing of cilantro.
7. Enjoy.

PARSLEY, Kale, and Tofu Brown Rice

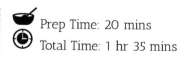

Prep Time: 20 mins
Total Time: 1 hr 35 mins

Servings per Recipe: 12	
Calories	289 kcal
Fat	11.3 g
Carbohydrates	39g
Protein	11.5 g
Cholesterol	0 mg
Sodium	770 mg

Ingredients

2 C. brown rice
4 C. water
1 (16 oz.) package extra firm tofu, diced
3/4 C. tamari almonds
1/4 C. sesame seeds
1 bunch kale, ribs removed, chopped
1/2 large head red cabbage, chopped
1 C. shredded carrot
1 C. chopped fresh flat-leaf parsley
1/2 C. chopped fresh dill

1/2 C. lemon juice
1/2 C. tamari soy sauce
2 tbsps extra-virgin olive oil
8 cloves garlic, chopped
1/4 C. stone-ground mustard
salt and ground black pepper to taste

Directions

1. Get your water and rice boiling then place a lid on the pot, set the heat to low and let the contents cook for 47 mins.
2. Add the rice to a bowl after a few mins and then put it in the fridge to get cold.
3. Meanwhile get a bowl, combine: mustard, lemon juice, olive oil, soy sauce, and garlic.
4. Take out your rice and add to the bowl: dill, tofu, parsley, almonds, carrots, sesame seeds, red cabbage, and kale.
5. Top the rice with the lemon dressing and stir everything. Enjoy.

Sweet
Brown Rice Chive Patties

Prep Time: 15 mins
Total Time: 30 mins

Servings per Recipe: 6
Calories	285 kcal
Fat	6.1 g
Carbohydrates	53.4g
Protein	9.9 g
Cholesterol	62 mg
Sodium	620 mg

Ingredients

2 (15.25 oz.) cans whole kernel sweet corn, drained
2 C. cooked brown rice, cooled
1/2 C. skim milk
2 eggs, beaten
2 tbsps chopped fresh chives
2/3 C. whole wheat flour

2 tsps baking powder
1/8 tsp ground nutmeg
salt and ground black pepper to taste
1 tbsp olive oil, or as needed

Directions

1. Get a bowl, mix: chives, corn, eggs, rice, and milk.
2. Get a 2nd bowl, mix: black pepper, flour, salt, baking powder, and nutmeg.
3. Combine both bowls then fry a quarter of a C. of mix in olive oil for 4 mins for each side.
4. Place on paper towel to drain excess oils.
5. Enjoy.

EASY
Hawaiian Style Brown Rice

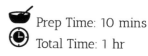

Prep Time: 10 mins
Total Time: 1 hr

Servings per Recipe: 6
Calories	352 kcal
Fat	9.7 g
Carbohydrates	46.8g
Protein	21.5 g
Cholesterol	102 mg
Sodium	1033 mg

Ingredients

2 C. Minute(R) Brown Rice, uncooked
1 (20 oz.) can crushed pineapple, divided
1 (20 oz.) package ground turkey or chicken
3/4 C. green onions, thinly sliced, divided

1/2 C. teriyaki sauce, divided
1 egg, lightly beaten
1 tsp ground ginger
1/2 tsp ground nutmeg
2 tbsps orange marmalade

Directions

1. Cook the rice in line with its associated directions then set your oven to 350 degrees before doing anything else.
2. Separate half a C. of pineapple juice for later.
3. Get a bowl, combine: nutmeg, ground meat, ginger, rice, half of the teriyaki, half of the pineapple, and half of the onions.
4. Shape the mix into balls.
5. Then layer them in a casserole dish coated with nonstick spray and cook everything in the oven for 27 mins.
6. Meanwhile simmer the following remaining ingredients for 5 mins: orange marmalade, pineapple and juice, onions, and teriyaki.
7. When the meatballs are done top with the sauce.
8. Enjoy

Mesa
Rice

🥣 Prep Time: 10 mins

🕐 Total Time: 40 mins

Servings per Recipe: 8	
Calories	465 kcal
Fat	33.7 g
Carbohydrates	21.1g
Protein	19.7 g
Cholesterol	89 mg
Sodium	747 mg

Ingredients

1 tbsp butter, or as needed
3 C. cooked rice, or more to taste
2 C. sour cream
1 lb shredded Monterey Jack cheese
2 (4 oz.) cans diced green chilies

1/2 C. grated Cheddar cheese
salt to taste

Directions

1. Coat a baking dish with butter and set your oven to 350 degrees before doing anything else.
2. Add to the baking dish the following (in order): rice, salt, sour cream, green chilies, and Monterey. Top with some cheddar.
3. Cook for 32 mins in the oven. Let the contents cool.
4. Enjoy.

BEEF
and Onion Rice

Prep Time: 15 mins
Total Time: 55 mins

Servings per Recipe: 6
Calories   269 kcal
Fat   10 g
Carbohydrates   35.9g
Protein   8.5 g
Cholesterol   20 mg
Sodium   792 m

Ingredients

1/4 C. butter
1 1/4 C. long-grain rice
2 (10.5 oz.) cans beef consommé
1/2 tsp salt
3/4 C. diced green onions

3/4 C. diced carrots
3/4 C. diced celery
1/4 C. sliced almonds

Directions

1. Set your oven to 375 degrees before doing anything else.
2. For 5 mins fry your rice in melted butter until toasted and browned. Add some salt and your consommé over the rice and get everything boiling. Once boiling enter the contents into a baking dish.
3. Cook the rice in the oven for 30 mins. Then add in come almonds, green onions, celery, and carrots to the rice and stir it nicely. Place it back in the oven for 5 more mins.
4. Enjoy.

Parsley
Butter Rice

🥣 Prep Time: 15 mins
🕐 Total Time: 50 mins

Servings per Recipe: 6
Calories	131 kcal
Fat	2.4 g
Carbohydrates	24.7g
Protein	2.4 g
Cholesterol	5 mg
Sodium	23 mg

Ingredients

1 tbsp butter
1 C. diced onion
1 clove garlic, minced
1 C. minced green bell pepper
3 1/3 C. water

1 1/2 C. converted rice
1/2 tsp dried parsley
1 bay leaf

Directions

1. Fry your onions for 5 mins in melted butter until see-through, in a saucepan.
2. Add the garlic into the onions and cook for another 3 mins.
3. Add in bell peppers and cook for 2 more mins.
4. Finally combine with the peppers and onions: water, bay leaf, parsley and rice.
5. Bring everything to a rolling boil and once boiling place a lid on the pot, set the heat to low, and then cook the rice for 22 mins until soft.
6. Let the contents cool for a bit.
7. Enjoy.

LATIN STYLE
Rice

Prep Time: 15 mins
Total Time: 35 mins

Servings per Recipe: 6
Calories	203 kcal
Fat	6.3 g
Carbohydrates	31.4g
Protein	4.1 g
Cholesterol	15 mg
Sodium	607 mg

Ingredients

3 tbsps butter
1 C. diced onions
1 C. diced green bell pepper
1/2 C. diced celery
1 clove garlic, minced
1 (28 oz.) can minced tomatoes with juice

2 tsps chili powder
2 tsps beef bouillon granules
1/2 tsp salt
3 C. cooked white rice

Directions

1. Stir fry the following in butter: garlic, onions, celery, and green bell peppers for 12 mins.
2. Add in your rice, salt, tomatoes with juice, beef bouillon, and chili powder.
3. Heat until lightly boiling and let the contents simmer for 22 mins until the rice is tender.
4. Enjoy.

Easy
Persian Style Rice

Prep Time: 10 mins

Total Time: 1 hr 20 mins

Servings per Recipe: 5

Calories	404 kcal
Fat	10.2 g
Carbohydrates	69.5g
Protein	7.1 g
Cholesterol	24 mg
Sodium	812 mg

Ingredients

2 C. uncooked long-grain rice
3/4 tsp crushed saffron threads
4 tbsps butter
6 whole cardamom seeds
4 whole cloves

3 cinnamon sticks
1 onion, chopped
3 C. boiling vegetable broth
1 tsp salt

Directions

1. Soak your rice in a bowl covered in cold water for 32 mins.
2. Get a 2nd bowl, and soak your saffron in 2 tbsps of boiling water.
3. Stir fry your cinnamon, cardamom, and cloves for 3 mins, then combine in onions and fry until they are browned. Once the onions are browned add in your rice and let it simmer for 7 mins.
4. Add in your broth at this point and let it boil.
5. Then add in your saffron water and some salt. Place a lid on the pan and set the heat to low and let the rice cook for 40 mins.

Easy Persian Style Rice

45

BACON, APPLES, and Mushroom White Rice

 Prep Time: 15 mins

Total Time: 45 mins

Servings per Recipe: 12
Calories	209 kcal
Fat	7 g
Carbohydrates	28.6g
Protein	8.4 g
Cholesterol	14 mg
Sodium	388 mg

Ingredients

3 C. water
1 1/2 C. uncooked white rice
3 slices turkey bacon
1/2 onion, chopped
2 stalks celery, diced
1 carrot, chopped
1/2 C. peas
1 C. fresh mushrooms, sliced
1/2 C. slivered almonds
1/2 C. raisins

1 Granny Smith apple - peeled, cored and diced
1 C. cooked, chopped turkey meat
1 tsp chicken soup base
3 tbsps soy sauce
1/2 C. chopped parsley
ground black pepper to taste

Directions

1. Get a large pot and get some water boiling in it. Then mix in your rice. Once boiling set the heat to low, place a lid on the pot and let the rice cook for 20 mins.
2. Fry your bacon until crispy and remove any excess oils. Then add in your apple, onions, raisins, celery, almonds, mushrooms, peas, and carrots. Continually stir over a lower heat until tender.
3. Finally add in the following: pepper, rice, turkey, parsley, chicken soup base, and soy sauce. Mix everything evenly. Enjoy.

Basmati
Peas and Peanut Rice

🥄 Prep Time: 10 mins
🕐 Total Time: 30 mins

Servings per Recipe: 4
Calories	302 kcal
Fat	9.5 g
Carbohydrates	45.7g
Protein	9 g
Cholesterol	0 mg
Sodium	318 mg

Ingredients

1 C. uncooked basmati rice
2 1/4 C. water
1/2 tsp salt
1/4 tsp ground turmeric

1/2 C. frozen petite peas, thawed
1/2 C. dry roasted peanuts

Directions

1. Bring the following to a rolling boil: turmeric, rice, salt, and water. Once boiling set the heat to low, place a lid on the pot, and let the rice cook for 22 mins.
2. After the cooking time has elapsed add in your peanuts and then your peas. Mix everything nicely.
3. Then serve once the peas have been warmed.

TEXAS
Cheddar Rice

 Prep Time: 30 mins

Total Time: 1 hr

Servings per Recipe: 10
Calories	391 kcal
Fat	17.4 g
Carbohydrates	33.9 g
Protein	22 g
Cholesterol	69 mg
Sodium	771 mg

Ingredients

3 C. water
2 C. uncooked long grain white rice
6 slices turkey bacon
1 1/2 lb ground beef
1 onion, chopped
1/2 green bell pepper, seeded and
chopped

1 (28 oz.) can peeled and diced tomatoes
1 1/2 tsps salt
1/4 tsp ground black pepper
1 1/2 C. shredded Cheddar cheese

Directions

1. Set your oven to 400 degrees before doing anything else.
2. Bring the following to a rolling boil: water and rice.
3. Set the heat to low and then place a lid on the pot and let the rice cook for 22 mins until tender.
4. Fry your bacon simultaneously until crispy.
5. Set aside 2 tbsps of oil. Then crumble the bacon.
6. Once the bacon is crumbled remove it from the pan and add in: onions, ground beef, and green peppers.
7. Cook everything until the beef is fully done.
8. Then remove all excess oils and add some pepper and salt for taste.
9. Now grab a casserole dish and put the rice and beef mix into it.
10. Then add bacon, beef mix, bacon oil, and tomatoes.
11. Combine everything nicely. Then garnish the dish with some cheddar. Cook in the oven for 35 mins. Enjoy.

West African Style Rice

🥣 Prep Time: 20 mins
🕐 Total Time: 1 hr 20 mins

Servings per Recipe: 8
Calories	332 kcal
Fat	13.4 g
Carbohydrates	33.5g
Protein	19.8 g
Cholesterol	46 mg
Sodium	713 mg

Ingredients

1 tbsp olive oil
1 large onion, sliced
2 (14.5 oz.) cans stewed tomatoes
1/2 (6 oz.) can tomato paste
1 tsp salt
1/4 tsp black pepper
1/4 tsp cayenne pepper
1/2 tsp red pepper flakes
1 tbsp Worcestershire sauce
1 tsp chopped fresh rosemary

2 C. water
1 (3 lbs) whole chicken, cut into 8 pieces
1 C. uncooked white rice
1 C. diced carrots
1/2 pound fresh green beans, trimmed and snapped into 1 to 2 inch pieces
1/4 tsp ground nutmeg

Directions

1. Fry your onions in oil until they are see-through.
2. Then add in tomato paste and tomato sauce, rosemary, salt, cayenne, red pepper flakes, and Worchestshire.
3. Bring everything to a rolling boil, then set the heat low, put in the water and the chicken pieces, and place a lid on the pot. Let the chicken simmer for 35 mins.
4. After 35 mins of simmering add in green beans, nutmeg, rice and carrots.
5. Get everything boiling again with high heat and then lower the heat.
6. Place a lid back on the pot and let the rice cook for 27 mins until soft. Enjoy.

CHILI
and Cilantro Jasmine

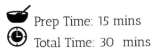

Prep Time: 15 mins
Total Time: 30 mins

Servings per Recipe: 4
Calories	634 kcal
Fat	17.3 g
Carbohydrates	84.4g
Protein	32.8 g
Cholesterol	68 mg
Sodium	562 mg

Ingredients

4 tbsps vegetable oil
5 cloves garlic, finely chopped
2 green chilies, diced
2 C. cubed skinless, boneless chicken
breast meat
2 C. cooked jasmine rice, chilled
1 tbsp white sugar

1 tbsp fish sauce
1 tbsp soy sauce
2 tsps chopped green onion
2 tbsps chopped fresh basil leaves
5 tbsps chopped fresh cilantro

Directions

1. Fry your garlic in a wok in oil and then add your chicken, and chili peppers. Stir fry until the chicken is fully cooked.
2. Once the chicken is cooked add in: soy sauce, sugar, rice, and fish sauce. Stir fry for 2 mins then add in your cilantro, green onions, and basil cook for another 2 mins. Then enjoy.

Texas
Ranch Style Basmati

🥘 Prep Time: 5 mins
🕐 Total Time: 30 mins

Servings per Recipe: 4
Calories	129.1
Fat	2.0g
Cholesterol	0.0mg
Sodium	294.4mg
Carbohydrates	25.6g
Protein	2.5g

Ingredients

1 tsp vegetable oil
2 tsp cilantro, chopped
2/3 C. white basmati rice
1 C. water

1/2 tsp salt
1 lime

Directions

1. In a 2-quart heavy pan, heat the oil over low heat and cook the rice and lime juice for about 1 minute, stirring continuously.
2. Stir in the salt and water and bring to a boil.
3. Reduce the heat to low and simmer, covered for about 25 minutes.
4. With a fork, fluff the rice and stir in the cilantro.
5. Serve immediately.

PUNJABI STYLE
Spicy Meatballs with Basmati

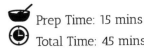 Prep Time: 15 mins
Total Time: 45 mins

Servings per Recipe: 6
Calories   306.4
Fat   11.2g
Cholesterol   0.0mg
Sodium   20.8mg
Carbohydrates   47.5g
Protein   6.0g

Ingredients

1/4 C. vegetable oil
1 onion, sliced
3 garlic cloves, peeled and chopped
1 C. water
1 tbsp grated ginger
1 tbsp garam masala
2 tsp ground coriander
1 tsp ground cumin
1 tsp chili powder
1/2 tsp turmeric powder

420 g chopped tomatoes
1 kg meatballs
1/4 C. coriander leaves, chopped
salt
Rice
1 1/2 C. basmati rice, rinsed
800 g chopped tomatoes
2 bay leaves
4 whole cardamom pods

Directions

1. In a heavy bottomed frying pan, heat the oil and sauté the onion until golden.
2. Add the ginger and garlic and sauté for about 1 minute. Stir in the spices and sauté for about 2-3 minutes.
3. Stir in the tomato, 1 C. of the water and salt and stir to combine.
4. Carefully, place the meatballs and cook, covered for about 5 minutes.
5. Uncover and cook for about 10 minutes. (You can add some water if sauce becomes too thick).
6. Meanwhile, for the rice: in a pan, add the rice, tomato, cardamom, bay leaves, salt and enough water to cover over medium heat and bring to a boil.
7. Reduce the heat to low and simmer, covered for about 15 minutes. Remove from the heat and keep aide, covered for about 10 minutes.
8. Serve the meatballs with a garnishing of the coriander alongside the rice.

Basmati
Marrakesh

Prep Time: 10 mins
Total Time: 35 mins

Servings per Recipe: 4
Calories	326.3
Fat	7.9g
Cholesterol	15.2mg
Sodium	48.3mg
Carbohydrates	53.6g
Protein	11.0g

Ingredients

1 C. basmati rice
2 C. vegetable broth
2 tbsp butter
1/2 C. red lentil
1/2 C. peas
2 tsp ground cumin

1/2 tsp curry powder
1 dash garam masala
1 dash coriander

Directions

1. In a pan, add the rice, butter and broth and simmer, covered for about 25 minutes.
2. Meanwhile, in a pan of the water, cook the lentils, covered for about 20 minutes.
3. Drain the lentils well.
4. In a steamer, steam the peas until desired doneness.
5. In a large serving bowl, add the rice, lentils, peas and spices and mix until well combined.
6. Serve immediately.

CARIBBEAN
Basmati Salad

Prep Time: 10 mins

Total Time: 25 mins

Servings per Recipe: 4

Calories	335.7
Fat	2.3g
Cholesterol	0.0mg
Sodium	7.0mg
Carbohydrates	73.9g
Protein	6.2g

Ingredients

1 1/2 C. white basmati rice, rinsed and drained
3/4 C. orange juice
6 tbsp lime juice
1 tbsp sugar
1 - 2 large mango, firm, ripe, peeled, and chopped

heaping 1/8 tsp nutmeg
salt
chopped parsley

Directions

1. In a pan, add the rice and 2 1/3 C. of the water over high heat and bring to a boil.
2. Reduce the heat to low and simmer, covered for about 15 minutes.
3. Remove from the heat and keep aide, uncovered to cool completely.
4. After cooling with a fork, fluff the rice.
5. In a large serving bowl, add the juices, sugar and nutmeg and mix until sugar is dissolved
6. Add the rice, mango, parsley and salt and stir to combine well.
7. Refrigerate to chill before serving.

Hot Sweet and Savory Basmati with Figs

Prep Time: 10 mins
Total Time: 30 mins

Servings per Recipe: 6
Calories   299.3
Fat   6.3g
Cholesterol   10.1mg
Sodium   32.6mg
Carbohydrates   55.3g
Protein   5.8g

Ingredients

2 tbsp butter
1 tbsp mustard seeds
1/2 C. onion, minced
1 tbsp ginger, minced
1 hot pepper, seeded and minced
2 C. basmati rice

salt
4 small firm figs, diced

Directions

1. In a heavy bottomed pan, melt the butter over medium heat and cook the onion, ginger, jalapeño and mustard seeds for about 4-5 minutes.
2. Add the rice and stir to combine well.
3. Add the figs, 3-1/2 C. of the water and salt and bring to a boil.
4. Reduce the heat to low and simmer, covered for about 10 minutes.
5. Remove from the heat and keep aide, covered for about 10 minutes.
6. Serve hot.

COUNTRY STYLE
Mushroom Basmati

 Prep Time: 10 mins
Total Time: 30 mins

Servings per Recipe: 6
Calories	231.7
Fat	5.2g
Cholesterol	7.3mg
Sodium	176.5mg
Carbohydrates	38.6g
Protein	10.4g

Ingredients

3 bunches kale, stems removed
1 C. water
1 1/2 tbsp red wine vinegar
1 1/2 tsp olive oil
1 C. chopped onion
2 garlic cloves, minced
1 (8 oz.) packet pre-sliced mushrooms
1 C. uncooked basmati rice
1 tsp dried basil
1 (14 1/2 oz.) cans vegetable broth

1 bay leaf
1/2 C. grated Parmesan cheese
1/4 tsp ground black pepper

Directions

1. In a large Dutch oven, add 1 C. of the water and bring to a boil.
2. Stir in the kale and cook for about 15 minutes.
3. Drain the kale well and keep side to cool slightly.
4. The, chop the kale and transfer into a bowl.
5. Drizzle the kale with the vinegar.
6. In a pan, heat the oil over medium heat and sauté the onion for about 3 minutes.
7. Stir in the mushrooms and garlic and sauté for about 2 minutes.
8. Add the rice and cook for about 1 minute, stirring frequently.
9. Stir in the basil, bay leaf and broth and bring to a boil.
10. Reduce the heat to low and simmer, covered for about 12 minutes.
11. Place the kale on top of the rice and simmer, covered for about 5 minutes.
12. Remove from the heat and discard the bay leaf.
13. Add the cheese and pepper and toss to coat well before serving.

Southern Italian
Style Basmati with Tomato Base

Prep Time: 10 mins
Total Time: 45 mins

Servings per Recipe: 4
Calories	793.5
Fat	40.0g
Cholesterol	0.0mg
Sodium	1018.6mg
Carbohydrates	99.6g
Protein	10.6g

Ingredients

2/3 C. vegetable oil
2 onions, sliced
1 tsp onion seeds
1 tsp ginger root, chopped
1 tsp crushed garlic
1/2 tsp turmeric

1 tsp chili powder
1 1/2 tsp salt
14 oz. canned tomatoes
2 1/2 C. basmati rice
2 1/2 C. water

Directions

1. In a pan, heat the oil over medium heat and sauté the onions for about 5 minutes.
2. Add the onion seeds, garlic, ginger, turmeric, chili powder and salt and mix well.
3. Reduce the heat and stir in the tomatoes.
4. Cook for about 10 minutes, breaking with the back of spoon.
5. Add the rice and gently stir to combine.
6. Add the water and stir to combine.
7. Reduce the heat to low and simmer, covered for about 10 minutes.

ARIZONA
Basmati

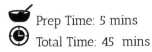 Prep Time: 5 mins

Total Time: 45 mins

Servings per Recipe: 2

Calories	394.2
Fat	8.4g
Cholesterol	15.2mg
Sodium	52.1mg
Carbohydrates	71.6g
Protein	7.4g

Ingredients

1 C. brown basmati rice
1/2 tbsp vegetable bouillon granules
2 C. boiling water

1 tbsp butter
1/2 jalapeño pepper, minced

Directions

1. In a small pan, melt the butter and sauté the jalapeño until softened.
2. Add the rice and cook for about 1 minute, stirring continuously.
3. Add the bouillon granules and water and bring to a boil.
4. Reduce the heat to low and simmer, covered for about 40 minutes.
5. Serve hot.

Tuesday's
Buttery Almond Basmati

Prep Time: 5 mins
Total Time: 25 mins

Servings per Recipe: 4
Calories	300.0
Fat	6.9 g
Cholesterol	5.0 mg
Sodium	26.9 mg
Carbohydrates	55.9 g
Protein	6.0 g

Ingredients

1 C. uncooked basmati rice
water
2 tsp butter
2 tsp cumin seeds
salt

3/4 C. mixed dried fruit, chopped
1/4 C. slivered almonds, toasted

Directions

1. Set your oven to 350 degrees F before doing anything else.
2. Arrange the almonds onto a metal baking sheet in a single layer.
3. Cook the rice with the butter, cumin seeds and salt according to package's instructions.
4. Cook in the oven for about 3-5 minutes, stirring occasionally.
5. Remove from the oven and keep aside to cool.
6. After cooking, spread the almonds and dried fruit on top and keep aside, loosely covered for about 10 minutes.
7. With a fork, fluff the rice and serve.

20-MINUTE
Rice Cooker Basmati

 Prep Time: 5 mins

Total Time: 20 mins

Servings per Recipe: 4

Calories	501.6
Fat	14.6g
Cholesterol	30.5mg
Sodium	769.3mg
Carbohydrates	81.6g
Protein	11.1g

Ingredients

2 C. basmati rice
4 C. water
4 tbsp butter
1 tbsp turmeric
1 tsp salt

2 C. frozen peas
cilantro

Directions

1. In the bowl of the rice cooker, add the rice, turmeric and salt and mixed until well combined.
2. Add the butter and water and set the rice cooker to cook.
3. Stir in the frozen peas and keep aside for a few minutes before serving.
4. Serve with a garnishing of the cilantro.

Vermicelli Pilaf

🥣 Prep Time: 15 mins

🕐 Total Time: 45 mins

Servings per Recipe: 8

Calories	204.1
Fat	4.2g
Cholesterol	0.0mg
Sodium	150.6mg
Carbohydrates	37.6g
Protein	3.9g

Ingredients

5 tsp olive oil
3/4 C. chopped sweet onion
2 C. uncooked basmati rice
3/4 C. uncooked vermicelli, broken into pieces
3 C. reduced-sodium fat-free chicken broth

1/2 tsp salt
1/4 tsp black pepper
1/4 C. chopped parsley
1/4 C. chopped green onion

Directions

1. Set your oven to 350 degrees F before doing anything else.
2. In a Dutch oven, heat the oil over medium heat and cook the sweet onion for about 3 minutes, stirring frequently.
3. Stir in the vermicelli and rice and cook for about 2 minutes, stirring frequently.
4. Stir in the broth, salt and black pepper and bring to a boil.
5. Immediately, cover the pan and transfer into the oven.
6. Cook in the oven for about 15 minutes.
7. Remove from the oven and keep aide, covered for about 15 minutes.
8. Stir in the green onions and parsley and serve.

PEPPERY
Pecan Basmati with Mushrooms

 Prep Time: 10 mins

Total Time: 30 mins

Servings per Recipe: 6
Calories	176.4
Fat	5.9g
Cholesterol	0.2mg
Sodium	486.4mg
Carbohydrates	27.8g
Protein	3.9g

Ingredients

2 garlic cloves, minced
2 tsp olive oil
1 C. basmati rice
2 tsp instant chicken bouillon granules
2 tsp lemon zest
4 oz. cremini mushrooms, sliced
4 green onions, sliced
1/4 C. red pepper, chopped

1/4 tsp salt
1/8 tsp black pepper
2 tbsp pecans, toasted and chopped
6 lemon slices

Directions

1. In a medium pan, heat the oil and sauté the garlic for about 30 seconds.
2. Stir in the rice, bouillon granules and water and bring to a boil.
3. Reduce the heat to low and simmer, covered for about 10 minutes.
4. Stir in the mushrooms, red peppers, green onions, lemon zest, salt and pepper and simmer, covered for about 10 minutes.
5. Stir in the pecans and remove from the heat.
6. Serve with a garnishing of the lemon slices.

Milanese
Basmati

Prep Time: 5 mins
Total Time: 30 mins

Servings per Recipe: 6
Calories	232.9
Fat	5.3g
Cholesterol	10.1mg
Sodium	617.6mg
Carbohydrates	42.0g
Protein	4.6g

Ingredients

1 1/2 C. basmati rice, rinsed
2 tbsp butter
2 C. sweet onions, chopped
2 1/2 C. water
1 1/2 tsp salt

3 tbsp parsley, chopped
2 tbsp dill, chopped
2 tbsp tarragon, chopped

Directions

1. In a large pan, melt the butter over medium-high heat and sauté the onions for about 5 minutes.
2. Stir in the rice, salt and water and bring to a boil.
3. Reduce the heat to low and simmer, covered for about 15 minutes.
4. Remove from the heat and keep aide, covered for about 10 minutes.
5. Season with the salt and black pepper and serve.

BASHIR'S
Basmati Pudding

 Prep Time: 15 mins
Total Time: 3 hrs 15 mins

Servings per Recipe: 8
Calories	171.1
Fat	4.5g
Cholesterol	12.2mg
Sodium	50.1mg
Carbohydrates	27.5g
Protein	5.3g

Ingredients

4 C. whole milk
1/3 C. demerara sugar
2 tsp ground cardamom

3/4 C. brown basmati rice, rinsed
chopped unsalted pistachio nuts

Directions

1. Lightly grease a 3 1/2-quart slow cooker.
2. In a large pan, add the milk over medium heat and bring to a boil, stirring occasionally.
3. Stir in the cardamom and sugar and remove from the heat.
4. Stir in the rice and transfer the mixture into a prepared slow cooker.
5. Arrange a folded tea towel on top of the slow cooker pot.
6. Set the slow cooker on High and cook, covered for about 3 hours.
7. Uncover and transfer the pudding into a serving bowl. Keep aside at room temperature to cool.
8. Serve with a garnishing of the pistachios.

European Cabbage Rolls

🥣 Prep Time: 1 hr
🕐 Total Time: 1 hr 45 mins

Servings per Recipe: 4
Calories   499.4
Fat   7.9g
Cholesterol   0.0mg
Sodium   2685.0mg
Carbohydrates   99.4g
Protein   16.0g

Ingredients

1 tbsp olive oil
1 tsp olive oil
1 C. onion, chopped
1/2 C. celery, chopped
1/2 C. red bell pepper, diced
3 C. mushrooms, sliced
1 garlic clove, minced

3 C. vegetable stock
1 1/2 C. basmati rice, uncooked
2 tbsp parsley
1 green cabbage, cored
2 lb. sauerkraut
3 1/2 C. tomato sauce

Directions

1. In a pan, heat the oil over medium-low heat and cook the bell pepper, onion, celery and salt, covered for about 5 minutes.
2. Add the mushrooms and garlic and cook, covered for about 5 minutes.
3. Add the rice, stock and pepper and stir to combine.
4. Increase the heat to high and bring to a boil.
5. Reduce the heat to low and simmer, covered for about 15 minutes.
6. With a fork, fluff the rice and stir in the parsley.
7. Meanwhile, in a large pan, add 1-inch of the water and bring to a boil.
8. Add the cabbage, cored side down and cook, covered for about 5 minutes.
9. With a slotted spoon, transfer the cabbage onto a platter and immediately, remove first 4 leaves.
10. With a plastic wrap, cover the leaves.
11. Place the cabbage into the pan again and repeat the process.
12. Let the leaves cool slightly.
13. Carefully, remove the tough ridge from center of leaves.
14. Set your oven to 375 degrees F.
15. In a colander, place the sauerkraut and keep aside to drain.

16. Rinse the sauerkraut under cold running water and squeeze out the liquid.
17. Arrange the cabbage leaves onto a smooth surface.
18. Place about 3/4 C. of the rice mixture in the middle of each leaf.
19. Carefully, fold each leaf around the rice mixture.
20. In the bottom of a 13x9-inch casserole dish, arrange the sauerkraut in an even layer, followed by 2 C. of the tomato sauce.
21. Arrange the cabbage rolls over tomato sauce, seam side down and spread remaining tomato sauce on top evenly.
22. With a piece of foil, cover the casserole dish and cook in the oven for about 45 minutes.

Turkey Basmati Bake

Prep Time: 5 mins
Total Time: 55 mins

Servings per Recipe: 6
Calories	614.5
Fat	38.8g
Cholesterol	166.7mg
Sodium	624.0mg
Carbohydrates	50.0g
Protein	18.2g

Ingredients

1 1/2 C. cooked wild rice
1 C. pecans, chopped and toasted
1/4 C. dried fruits, chopped e.g. apricots,
cranberries and currants
6 tbsp butter
butter
6 tbsp flour
3 C. milk
1 tsp salt

salt
1/2 tsp ground black pepper
1/2 tsp Cajun spices
3 egg yolks, slightly beaten
2 C. roast turkey breast, shredded
1 C. Gruyere cheese, grated
1/4 C. cheddar cheese, grated

Directions

1. Set your oven to 350 degrees F before doing anything else and lightly, grease a 13x9-inch baking dish with some melted butter.

2. In a bowl, add the wild rice, basmati rice, dried fruit, pecans, salt and pepper and mix until well combined.

3. For sauce: in a medium pan, melt 6 tbsp of the butter and add the flour, beating continuously.

4. Cook for about 2 minutes, stirring continuously.

5. Slowly, add the milk, beating continuously.

6. Cook for about 4-6 minutes, stirring frequently.

7. Add the egg yolks, 1/2 tsp of Essence, salt and 1/2 tsp of pepper and beat until well combined.

8. In the bottom of the prepared baking dish, place half of the rice mixture, followed by half of the turkey and half of the sauce.

9. Repeat the layers and sprinkle with the both cheeses.

10. Cook in the oven for about 40-45 minutes.

PERSIAN
Pomegranate Rice Salad

 Prep Time: 10 mins

Total Time: 25 mins

Servings per Recipe: 6
Calories	230.5
Fat	8.4g
Cholesterol	0.0mg
Sodium	393.9mg
Carbohydrates	36.3g
Protein	4.2g

Ingredients

2 C. water
1 C. basmati rice
1 tsp salt
1/4 C. white wine vinegar
2 tsp grated orange rind
1/4 C. orange juice
1 1/2 tbsp olive oil
pepper

3 seedless oranges
1/2 C. pomegranate seeds
1/4 C. toasted pine nuts
3 tbsp chopped parsley

Directions

1. In a pan, add the water and bring to a boil.
2. Add the rice and salt and stir to combine.
3. Reduce the heat to low and simmer, covered for about 15 minutes.
4. Remove from the heat and keep aide, covered for about 5 minutes.
5. With a fork, fluff the rice and keep aside to cool.
6. In a large serving bowl, add the cooked rice, pomegranate, oranges, parsley and pine nuts and mix.
7. In another bowl, add the orange rind, orange juice, vinegar, oil, salt and pepper and beat until well combined.
8. Pour the dressing over the rice salad and toss to coat well.

Cinnamon
Sugar Basmati

🍲 Prep Time: 15 mins
🕐 Total Time: 40 mins

Servings per Recipe: 4
Calories	514.1
Fat	19.8g
Cholesterol	0.0mg
Sodium	589.5mg
Carbohydrates	76.5g
Protein	7.6g

Ingredients

2 C. basmati rice, soaked and rinsed
1 medium onion, chopped
6 cloves
6 -8 green cardamoms, split
1 cinnamon stick

1 tsp cumin seed
2 tsp brown sugar
5 tbsp sunflower oil
1 tsp marine salt

Directions

1. In a cast iron pan, heat the oil and sauté the onion for about 15 minutes, stirring frequently.
2. Stir in the cardamoms, cinnamon and cloves and cook until the cloves begin to swell.
3. Add the sugar and cook until sugar is caramelized, stirring continuously.
4. Sir in the cumin and cook for about 1 minute, stirring continuously.
5. Add the rice and stir to combine well.
6. Add enough boiling water to cover the rice by 1/3-inch.
7. Stir in the salt and increase the heat to high.
8. Cover the pan and cook for about 2 minutes.
9. Reduce the heat to medium and cook for about 3 minutes.
10. Reduce the heat to low and simmer, covered for about 10 minutes.
11. Remove from the heat and keep aide, covered for about 5 minutes.
12. Discard the whole spices and serve.

AMERICAN
Basmati Chili

 Prep Time: 15 mins

Total Time: 45 mins

Servings per Recipe: 4	
Calories	472.4
Fat	4.9g
Cholesterol	49.9mg
Sodium	175.8mg
Carbohydrates	74.1g
Protein	33.7g

Ingredients

Chili
vegetable oil cooking spray
1 C. onion, chopped
3/4 tsp garlic, minced
3/4 tsp chopped ginger root
1/2 jalapeño pepper, chopped
3 oz. mushrooms, chopped
2 tsp flour
11 oz. boneless skinless chicken breasts, cubed
1 1/4 lb. canned white beans, drained and rinsed
1 1/4 C. organic low sodium chicken broth
3/4 tsp dried oregano leaves
3/4 tsp ground cumin
1/4 tsp ground coriander
1/8 tsp ground cinnamon
3/4 bay leaf

Toppings
3/4 small tomatoes
1 1/4 green onions, sliced
1 tbsp green olives
1 tsp green olives
1 tbsp finely chopped cilantro
1 tsp chopped cilantro
guacamole
sour cream
salsa
corn tortilla strips
Rice
2 C. water
1 C. basmati rice
1/8 tsp saffron

Directions

1. Grease a large pan with the cooking spray and heat over medium heat.
2. Add the onion, ginger, garlic and jalapeño and sauté for about 5 minutes.
3. Stir in the mushrooms and cook, covered for about 5 minutes.
4. Stir in the flour and cook for about 1 minute, stirring continuously.
5. Stir in the chicken, beans, herbs and chicken broth and bring to a boil.
6. Reduce the heat to low and simmer, covered for about 10-15 minutes.

7. Stir in salt and black pepper and remove from the heat.
8. Discard the bay leaf.
9. Meanwhile, for the rice: in a pan, add the water over high heat and bring to a boil.
10. Add the rice and saffron and stir to combine.
11. Reduce the heat to low and simmer, covered for about 15-20 minutes.
12. Remove from the heat and keep aide, covered for about 5 minutes.
13. With a fork, fluff the rice and serve.
14. Divide the chili into serving bowls and serve with a garnishing of the tomato, olives, green onion and cilantro alongside the rice, guacamole, sour cream, salsa and tortilla strips.

3-INGREDIENT
Cajun Basmati

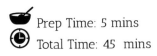 Prep Time: 5 mins

Total Time: 45 mins

Servings per Recipe: 1
Calories	1465.3
Fat	67.3g
Cholesterol	129.3mg
Sodium	2762.2mg
Carbohydrates	152.5g
Protein	58.0g

Ingredients

1/2 lb. andouille sausages, sliced
1 C. basmati rice, rinsed in cold water
2 C. water

Directions

1. In a 10-inch skillet, add the sausage slices and 1/2 C. of the water over medium heat and cook, covered for about 15 minutes.
2. Uncover and cook the sausage until all the liquid is absorbed.
3. Add the rice and stir fry until browned.
4. Stir in the remaining water and bring to a boil.
5. Reduce the heat to low and simmer, covered for about 10-12 minutes.
6. Remove from the heat and keep aide, covered for about 30 minutes.
7. With a fork, fluff the rice and serve.

Full
Basmati Rice Platter

🥣 Prep Time: 20 mins
🕐 Total Time: 1 hr 20 mins

Servings per Recipe: 8
Calories	279.2
Fat	0.0mg
Cholesterol	32.1mg
Sodium	36.1g
Carbohydrates	4.9g

Ingredients

1 1/2 C. basmati rice, rinsed
kosher salt, if desired
Toppings
1/2 C. dried onion flakes, toasted in a little oil
1/4 C. toasted slivered almonds, pan-toasted in a little ghee
1/4 C. toasted cashew nuts, pan-toasted in a little ghee

1/4 C. currants
silver aluminum foil
Fried Okra
1/4 lb. okra, trimmed and sliced
5 tbsp light vegetable oil
1 tsp lemon juice

Directions

1. In a large bowl of the water, soak the rice for about 30 minutes.
2. Meanwhile, for the okra: in a large frying pan, heat the oil over high heat. Arrange the okra slices in a single layer and reduce the heat to medium. Cook for about 20 minutes, flipping occasionally.
3. Stir in the lemon juice and remove from the heat.
4. With a slotted spoon, transfer the okra onto the paper towels-lined plate to drain. Drain the rice well.
5. In a pan, add 12 C. of the water and salt and bring to a boil.
6. Stir in the rice and again bring to a boil.
7. Cook the rice for about 4 minutes.
8. Drain the rice well. Transfer the rice into a greased 2-quart bowl and press to pack into the bowl.
9. Carefully, invert the rice onto a platter.
10. Serve with a decoration of onion flakes, crispy okra, currants and nuts.

30-MINUTE
Basmati Pilaf

Prep Time: 5 mins
Total Time: 30 mins

Servings per Recipe: 4

Calories	206.2
Fat	4.8g
Cholesterol	0.0mg
Sodium	586.6mg
Carbohydrates	36.7g
Protein	3.7g

Ingredients

1 tbsp canola oil
3 inches piece cinnamon sticks, halved
2 green cardamom pods
2 whole cloves
1/4 C. sliced onion

1 C. basmati rice
1 tsp table salt
1 1/2 C. water

Directions

1. In a medium pan, heat the oil and sauté the whole spices until they pop.
2. Add the onions and cook for about 2 minutes, stirring frequently.
3. Add the rice and cook for about 1 minute, stirring continuously.
4. Stir in the water and salt and bring to a boil.
5. Reduce the heat to low and simmer, covered for about 17 minutes.
6. Remove from the heat and keep aide, covered for about 10 minutes.
7. With a fork, fluff the rice and serve

Azza's
Basmati Salad

🥄 Prep Time: 20 mins

🕐 Total Time: 40 mins

Servings per Recipe: 6
Calories	279.8
Fat	14.3g
Cholesterol	0.0mg
Sodium	304.7mg
Carbohydrates	34.6g
Protein	4.7g

Ingredients

Base
1 1/4 C. uncooked brown basmati rice, rinsed
1/2 tsp salt
2 - 3 stalks celery, chopped
100 g dried cranberries
1/2 C. walnuts, chopped
Dressing
2 tbsp peanut oil

1 tbsp walnut oil
1 1/2 tbsp sherry wine vinegar
2 tsp ginger, grated
1 - 2 tsp liquid honey
1/4 tsp salt
1/4 tsp pepper

Directions

1. In a pan, add the rice, salt and required amount of the boiling water and cook according to the package's directions.
2. In a sieve, rinse the cooked rice with running cold water.
3. Drain completely and transfer into a bowl.
4. Add the cranberries, celery and walnuts and mix.
5. For the vinaigrette: in a bowl, add all the ingredients and beat until well combined.
6. Pour the vinaigrette over the rice salad and gently, toss to coat.

GINGER
Basmati with Eggplant

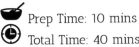

Prep Time: 10 mins
Total Time: 40 mins

Servings per Recipe: 4
Calories	555.7
Fat	20.1g
Cholesterol	41.6mg
Sodium	1857.0mg
Carbohydrates	84.4g
Protein	14.7g

Ingredients

Veggies
1/4 C. ghee
1/2 C. onion, chopped
3 garlic cloves, chopped
1 tsp cumin seed
1/2 tsp mustard seeds
1 tbsp ginger, grated
1 fresh jalapeño pepper
1 eggplant, cubed
1 bunch spinach, rinsed
4 tomatoes, chopped
1 tsp turmeric
1 1/2 tsp salt

15 oz. garbanzo beans
1 tbsp lemon juice, fresh
1 tbsp sugar
Rice
1 C. white basmati rice, rinsed
2 C. water
1 tsp salt
1 tsp turmeric
1 tbsp ginger , grated
1 tbsp ghee

Directions

1. For the Vegetables: in a large soup pan, melt the ghee over medium-high heat and cook the onions, ginger, garlic, jalapeño, cumin seeds and mustard seeds until the onions are translucent.

2. Stir in the eggplant and cook for about 8 minutes, stirring occasionally. Add the spinach and cook, covered for a few minutes.

3. Stir in the tomatoes, turmeric and salt and cook for about 10 minutes. Add the garbanzo beans, sugar and lemon juice and cook for about 5 minutes. Meanwhile, for the spiced rice: in a pan, add the water and bring to a rolling boil.

4. Add the rice, ghee, and spices and mix well. Reduce the heat to low and simmer, covered for about 25-30 minutes. Remove from the heat and keep aide, covered for about 5 minutes.

5. With a fork, fluff the rice and serve alongside the stew.

Ginger Basmati with Eggplant

Karachi Style
Chicken Salad

Prep Time: 40 mins
Total Time: 1 hr 5 mins

Servings per Recipe: 6
Calories	390.9
Fat	11.1g
Cholesterol	39.6mg
Sodium	650.0mg
Carbohydrates	51.2g
Protein	23.0g

Ingredients

Base
1 1/2 C. water
1 C. uncooked basmati rice
3 garlic cloves, minced
2 C. shredded rotisserie cooked boneless skinless chicken breasts
1/2 C. sliced green onion
1/4 C. chopped drained sun-dried tomato
1 tsp grated lemon rind
1 (15 1/2 oz.) cans chickpeas, rinsed and drained
1 (14 oz.) cans artichoke hearts, drained and chopped

Dressing
1/4 C. fat-free chicken broth
3 tbsp lemon juice
3 tbsp extra virgin olive oil
1 tsp Dijon mustard
3/4 tsp salt
1/2 tsp ground black pepper
1/4 tsp dried oregano

Directions

1. For the salad: in a 3-quart pan, add the water and bring to a boil.
2. Add the rice and garlic and stir to combine.
3. Reduce the heat to low and simmer, covered for about 20 minutes.
4. Remove from the heat and keep aide, covered for about 5 minutes.
5. Transfer the rice into a large bowl.
6. Add the chicken, green onion, sun-dried tomato, lemon rind, chickpeas and artichoke hearts and gently, stir to combine.
7. For the dressing: in a bowl, add all ingredients and beat until well combined.
8. Pour the dressing over the rice salad and gently, toss to coat.

BASMATI
Kerala

 Prep Time: 5 mins
Total Time: 50 mins

Servings per Recipe: 4
Calories	182.9
Fat	1.4g
Cholesterol	0.0mg
Sodium	16.3mg
Carbohydrates	38.3g
Protein	4.0g

Ingredients

1 C. brown basmati rice, rinsed and
drained
2 C. water
1 tbsp dried onion flakes
1/4 C. julienne carrot
1/4 C. diced celery
1/4 C. diced red bell pepper

1 tsp season salt
1/2 tsp dried jalapeño pepper
1/2 tsp cumin

Directions

1. In a medium pan, add the water over high heat and bring to a boil.
2. Add the rice and remaining ingredients and cook according to package's directions.

Ginger Garlic
Basmati with Squash

Prep Time: 10 mins
Total Time: 30 mins

Servings per Recipe: 8
Calories	247.5
Fat	9.0g
Cholesterol	20.3mg
Sodium	390.9mg
Carbohydrates	39.0g
Protein	4.2g

Ingredients

1 lb. butternut squash, peeled, seeded and cut into cubes
2 C. minced onions
3 tbsp minced ginger
1 tbsp minced garlic
1/3 C. butter
1 1/2 C. basmati rice, rinsed and drained

1 1/2 tbsp curry powder
1/2 tsp salt
3 C. de-fatted chicken broth
2 tbsp chopped cilantro

Directions

1. In a 5-6-quart pan, melt the butter over medium heat and cook onions, garlic and ginger for about 10-15 minutes, stirring frequently.
2. Add the rice and cook for about 5 minutes, stirring occasionally.
3. Add the curry powder and cook for about 30 seconds, stirring continuously.
4. Stir in the squash, broth and 1/2 tsp of the salt and bring to a boil over high heat.
5. Reduce the heat to low and simmer, covered for about 16-18 minutes, stirring occasionally.
6. Stir in the cilantro and salt and serve.

60-MINUTE
Basmati

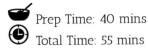 Prep Time: 40 mins

Total Time: 55 mins

Servings per Recipe: 6
Calories	265.7
Fat	6.3g
Cholesterol	0.0mg
Sodium	5.6mg
Carbohydrates	47.1g
Protein	4.9g

Ingredients

350 g basmati rice, rinsed
2 cloves
1 inch cinnamon stick
2 bay leaves
3 green cardamom pods
1 1/2 tsp cumin seeds
Onions

2 tbsp vegetable oil
1 onion, sliced
2 tbsp chopped coriander

Directions

1. In a large bowl of the water, soak the rice for about 30 minutes.
2. Drain the rice well.
3. In a pan, add a liter of water and bring to a boil.
4. Add the rice and whole spices and boil for about 5-8 minutes.
5. Drain the rice and keep aside, covered.
6. In a frying pan, heat the oil and fry the onion for about 5-10 minutes or until crispy.
7. Transfer the onion onto a paper towel-lined plate to drain.
8. Serve the rice with a topping of the crispy onions and coriander.

Topical
Chutney with Basmati

Prep Time: 15 mins
Total Time: 15 mins

Servings per Recipe: 1
Calories	507.2
Fat	14.1g
Cholesterol	24.4mg
Sodium	1078.2mg
Carbohydrates	82.3g
Protein	13.9g

Ingredients

Chutney Spice
1 C. dry roasted channa dal
4 C. dry coconut powder
3 tsp kosher salt
2 tsp whole cumin seeds
2 tsp Indian red chili powder
Rice

2 C. basmati rice, rinsed and drained
4 C. water
4 tbsp unsalted butter

Directions

1. In a spice grinder, grind the roasted channa dal until a fine powder is formed.
2. Heat a cast iron skillet and roast the cumin seeds for about 3-5 minutes, stirring continuously. Remove from the heat and keep aside. In a food processor, add 2 C. of the coconut powder, channa dal powder, cumin seeds, chili powder and salt and pulse until powdered nicely.
3. Transfer the coconut mixture into a bowl with the remaining 2 C. of the coconut powder and stir to combine.
4. Transfer in an air-tight container to store.
5. In a pan, add the rice and water and bring to a boil.
6. Reduce the heat to low and simmer, covered for until the liquid is absorbed.
7. Uncover and with a fork, fluff the rice.
8. Again, cover the pan and cook for about 5 minutes.
9. Remove from the heat and gently, stir in the butter until melted.
10. Add 1/2 C. of the coconut powder mixture and toss to coat well.
11. Serve hot.

BACKYARD
Tandoori

Prep Time: 10 mins
Total Time: 8 hrs 55 mins

Servings per Recipe: 8
Calories   349 kcal
Fat   20.5 g
Carbohydrates   5.4g
Protein   34.2 g
Cholesterol   120 mg
Sodium   618 mg

Ingredients

2 (6 oz.) containers plain yogurt
2 tsp kosher salt
1 tsp black pepper
1/2 tsp ground cloves
2 tbsp freshly grated ginger
3 cloves garlic, minced
4 tsp paprika

2 tsp ground cumin
2 tsp ground cinnamon
2 tsp ground coriander
16 chicken thighs
olive oil spray

Directions

1. In a bowl, add the yogurt, salt, pepper, cloves, ginger, garlic, paprika, cumin, cinnamon and coriander and mix till well combined.
2. Rinse the chicken under cold water and with the paper towels, pat dry.
3. In a large resealable plastic bag, add the chicken thighs and yogurt mixture.
4. Seal the bag after squeezing out the excess air.
5. Shake the bag to coat evenly.
6. Refrigerate for about 8 hours or overnight, flipping the bag occasionally.
7. Set your outdoor grill for direct medium heat.
8. Remove the chicken from the bag and discard the marinade.
9. With the paper towels, wipe off the excess marinade.
10. Spray the chicken pieces with the olive oil spray.
11. Cook the chicken thighs on the grill for about 2 minutes per side.
12. Now, arrange the chicken thighs over the indirect heat and cook for about 35-40 minutes.

Classical
Korma

🥣 Prep Time: 20 mins
🕐 Total Time: 1 hr

Servings per Recipe: 4
Calories	398 kcal
Fat	27.5 g
Carbohydrates	13.4g
Protein	25.3 g
Cholesterol	95 mg
Sodium	477 mg

Ingredients

1/4 C. cashew halves
1/4 C. boiling water
3 cloves garlic, peeled
1 (1/2 inch) piece fresh ginger root, peeled and chopped
3 tbsp vegetable oil
2 bay leaves, crumbled
1 large onion, minced
1 tsp ground coriander
1 tsp garam masala
1 tsp ground cumin

1 tsp ground turmeric
1 tsp chili powder
3 skinless, boneless chicken breast halves - diced
1/4 C. tomato sauce
1 C. chicken broth
1/2 C. heavy cream
1/2 C. plain yogurt
1 tsp cornstarch, mixed with equal parts water

Directions

1. In a small bowl, soak the cashews in the boiling water for about 15-20 minutes.
2. In a food processor, add the garlic and ginger and pulse till smooth.
3. In a wok, heat the oil on medium heat and sauté the bay leaves for about 30 seconds.
4. Stir in the onion and cook for about 3-5 minutes.
5. Stir in the garlic paste, coriander, garam masala, cumin, turmeric and chili powder.
6. Stir in the chicken and cook for about 5 minutes.
7. Stir in the tomato sauce and chicken broth.
8. Reduce the heat and simmer, covered for about 15 minutes, stirring occasionally.
9. Meanwhile in a food processor, add the cashews with the soaking water, cream and yogurt and pulse till smooth.
10. Stir the cashew mixture in the curry and simmer for about 15 minutes, stirring occasionally.
11. Stir in the cornstarch mixture and cook for about 1-2 minutes.

APPLE
Chicken Curry

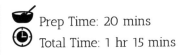 Prep Time: 20 mins

Total Time: 1 hr 15 mins

Servings per Recipe: 6

Calories	298 kcal
Fat	8.9 g
Carbohydrates	14.2g
Protein	38.8 g
Cholesterol	111 mg
Sodium	322 mg

Ingredients

3 tbsp butter
2 small onion, chopped
2 apples - peeled, cored and finely chopped
3 tbsp all-purpose flour
1 tbsp curry powder
8 skinless, boneless chicken breasts

1 C. hot chicken broth
1 C. milk
salt and pepper to taste

Directions

1. Set your oven to 350 degrees F before doing anything else.
2. In a pan, melt the butter on medium heat and sauté the apple till tender.
3. Add the curry powder and sauté for about 1 minute.
4. Stir in the flour and cook for about 1 minute.
5. Stir in the broth and milk and remove from the heat.
6. Season the chicken breasts with the salt and pepper evenly.
7. Arrange the chicken breasts in a 13x9-inch baking dish in a single layer.
8. Place the apple mixture over the chicken breasts evenly.
9. Cook in the oven for about 45-50 minutes.

Tuesday's Curry

🥣 Prep Time: 15 mins
🕐 Total Time: 1 hr 15 mins

Servings per Recipe: 4
Calories	286 kcal
Fat	9.9 g
Carbohydrates	14.9g
Protein	31.1 g
Cholesterol	88 mg
Sodium	620 mg

Ingredients

4 skinless, boneless chicken breast halves
2 tbsp butter
1 onion, chopped
2/3 C. beer
1 (10.75 oz.) can condensed tomato soup
1 tsp curry powder
1/2 tsp dried basil

1/2 tsp ground black pepper
1/4 C. grated Parmesan cheese

Directions

1. Set your oven to 350 degrees F before doing anything else.
2. In a medium skillet, melt the butter on medium heat and sauté the onion till tender.
3. Stir in the beer, soup, curry powder, basil and pepper.
4. Reduce the heat to low and simmer for about 10 minutes.
5. Arrange the chicken breasts in a 13x9-inch baking dish in a single layer.
6. Place the onion mixture over the chicken breasts evenly.
7. Cook in the oven for about 50 minutes.
8. Sprinkle with the cheese and cook in the oven for about 10 minutes.

CHICKEN
Curry 101

Prep Time: 10 mins
Total Time: 30 mins

Servings per Recipe: 6
Calories	343 kcal
Fat	24.3 g
Carbohydrates	9.8g
Protein	22.3 g
Cholesterol	62 mg
Sodium	83 mg

Ingredients

1 (3 lb.) whole chicken, skin removed
and cut into pieces
3 onions, chopped
1 tsp ground cinnamon
1 bay leaf
2 cloves crushed garlic
1/4 tsp ground ginger
1 tsp paprika
3 tbsp curry powder

1/2 tsp white sugar
1/2 lemon, juiced
1/2 tsp cayenne pepper
1 tbsp tomato paste
1 pinch salt
1/4 C. olive oil
water to cover

Directions

1. In a large skillet, heat the oil on medium heat and sauté the onion till browned.
2. Add the cinnamon, bay leaf, ginger, paprika, curry powder, sugar, salt and garlic and sauté for about 2 minutes.
3. Add the chicken pieces, tomato and enough water to just cover the chicken and simmer for about 20 minutes.
4. Stir in the lemon juice and the cayenne pepper and simmer for about 5 minutes.

Printed in Great Britain
by Amazon